Sock Loom

BASICS { using the KB Sock Loom }

MW00809126

Everyone loves hand-knitted socks! And now you can knit custom socks for everyone on your gift list—even if you've never knitted anything before! The adjustable KB Sock Loom* makes it easy. Just move the center adjustable slider pegs to the desired setting, and create the perfect size sock. You'll love making all the great designs in this book! The exciting patterns range from tiny socks for preemie babies to roomy socks for large adults. They include Mock Cable Socks, Beaded Socks, and Pedicure Socks for women; Ribbed Socks for men; and even a tiny Preemie Hat—11 styles in all. Along with the patterns, we've included some handy tips to make your Sock Loom experience even easier. With the complete instructions for the Sock Loom and all the projects right here in these pages, you'll be an expert in no time!

Discover the fun of knitting original gifts for everyone—the KB Sock Loom makes it easy!

*Your sock loom kit comes with a detailed DVD to get you started!

Table of Contents

LEISURE ARTS, INC.
Maumelle, Arkansas

basic knitting
instructions

First, we'll take you through our step-by-step instructions and then we'll get you started with the basic sock, page 5.

casting on

To begin knitting your sock start by putting stitches on the loom, or casting on.

To cast on, position your KB Sock Loom with one long side facing you and the wing nut on the opposite side.

Always cast on your first stitch beginning with the starting peg.
The starting peg is on the long side, facing you, adjacent to the slider pegs.

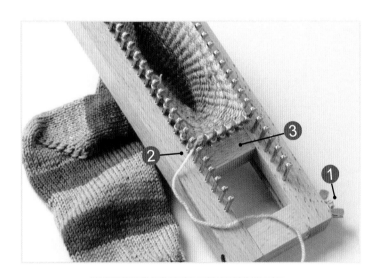

1. Wing nut
2. Starting peg
3. Adjustable slider pegs

E-wrap Cast On

1. Tie a slip knot onto the starting peg. Working in a counter clockwise motion, wrap each peg around.

2. To finish the cast on, wrap each peg one more time to create two loops on each peg.

3. Work these stitches by lifting the bottom loop over the top, leaving one loop on peg.

Here's another cast on method that's great if you find the yarn jumps off the pegs during the e-wrap. It creates a smooth top edge of the sock.

Begin with the slip knot on the starting peg. *Keep the working yarn to the front of the loom during the entire cast on.*

Insert crochet hook into the slip knot from top of loop.

Grab working yarn and pull to back of peg through the slip knot creating a loop. Place the loop over the second peg.

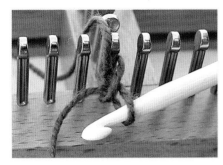

Insert the crochet hook from the inside, under the working yarn between peg 1 and 2.

Grab the working yarn, pull it to the back and loop it over the next empty peg to left.

Insert the crochet hook under the working yarn between peg 2 and 3.

Grab the working yarn and loop it over the next empty peg to left.

Continue grabbing the working yarn and looping it over the next empty peg around to the starting peg. Each peg should have 2 loops except the starting peg. Work an e-wrap on the starting peg.

Lift the bottom loop over the top loop and off the each peg around. Only one loop should remain on each peg. Now you are ready to begin the cuff!

The Flat Stitch is a tight stitch that is fast and easy to make. (The Knit Stitch and Flat Stitch are interchangeable.)

Hold the working yarn above loops on pegs. Lift loops over the working yarn and off the pegs.

Hint: When using the flat stitch, it is important to make sure that you do not pull the working yarn too tightly. If you do, the stitches will be very difficult to lift over. Allow plenty of yarn for each stitch before moving on.

Knit Stitch (KS): The Knit Stitch is similar to the Flat Stitch but is more stretchy.
Hold working yarn above loops. Insert hook from bottom to top of loop. Grab the working yarn and pull under loop and off the peg. Place the new loop onto same peg, leaving one loop on peg.

Purl Stitch (PS): The Purl stitch is used alone or with knit stitch to form ribbing for cuff.
Hold working yarn below loops. Insert hook from top to bottom of loop. Grab the working yarn and pull under loop and off the peg. Place the new loop onto same peg, leaving one loop on peg.

Wrap: Used to change direction of knitting when working short rows for the Heel and Toe.
Lift loop off peg and hold working yarn around back of peg. Place loop back onto same peg, creating one loop and one wrap on peg. Now your working yarn is below the loop.

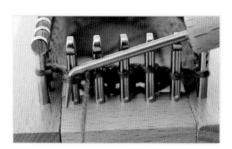

basic sock
instructions

This simple design is the best way to begin using the KB Sock Loom. You'll be surprised at how easy it is!

materials

Knitting Loom: KB Sock Loom

Stitches: FS, KS and PS

Yarn: 218 yards of fingering weight yarn. **SUPER FINE 1** Knit Picks Felici Fingering Self Striping Sock yarn was used in sample.

Notions: Knitting tool, Tapestry needle, (2) pieces of contrasting color yarn, each 10" long (optional) for closing toe.

GAUGE: 7 stitches and 12 rounds = 1" in FS.

CUFF

To determine the number of pegs to Cast on, see Sizing, page 7. Work in Rib pattern by knitting a combination of Knit or Flat Stitches and Purl Stitches. Cast on a multiple of 4 stitches. Work 2 Knit or Flat Stitches and 2 Purl and repeat those stitches around until the Cuff is the desired length.

A simple cuff will use the flat stitch around all pegs for a flat, rolled cuff. This cuff can also be hemmed for a flat, smooth cuff.

To Make a Hemmed Cuff, work in Flat Stitch for 1". Lift the cast on stitches onto the pegs from inside, one stitch at a time, leaving 2 loops on each peg. Lift the bottom loop over the top of each peg creating the hem.

LEG

The Leg is worked around in pattern until the you have reached the desired length. For the Basic Sock we knit every stitch around. The Leg length may be approximately 6" for shorter leg to 8" for longer leg.

HEEL

The Heel is worked using a technique called short rows, where you work back and forth instead of working in the round, using half the number of pegs required for the Leg. Only the pegs on one long side and the short, stationary side are worked.

1. Beginning at the starting peg, work around to the last peg on the short side. Do not work this last peg.

2. Wrap the last peg then work around to the starting peg. Do not work the starting peg.

3. Wrap the starting peg. Then work around to the last peg before the wrapped peg on the short side. Wrap this peg.

4. Work back across to the peg before the wrapped peg. Wrap this peg.

5. Continue working back and forth stopping at the peg before the wrapped peg, and wrapping that peg, until you have wrapped two-thirds of the heel pegs.

⑥ The next step of the Heel is to work the wrapped stitches.

⑦ Work the unwrapped, middle stitches around to the first wrapped stitches.

⑧ Knit the first wrapped stitch by lifting both the stitch and the wrapped loop over the working yarn.

⑨ Wrap the next peg, leaving 3 loops on this peg.

⑩ Work back across to the next wrapped peg. Work the wrapped stitch making sure to lift both the stitch and wrap off the peg. Wrap the next stitch being careful to get all loops back on the peg. Continue working all stitches back and forth until the last wrapped stitch on the short side.

⑪ Knit the last stitch then wrap the next stitch on the opposite side, leaving 2 stitches on the peg.

⑫ Work around to the starting peg, knit the first stitch then wrap the adjacent peg on short side.

Example: For socks with 30 Leg stitches, work the Heel on half the number of stitches required for the Leg or 15 stitches. Then, continue working the Heel until the first and last 5 stitches are wrapped and the middle 5 stitches are unwrapped.

The number of Heel stitches worked doesn't always divide out equally for the 3 sections. For example, if 22 Heel stitches are worked, the first and last 7 pegs would be wrapped, and the middle 8 pegs unwrapped.

Note: When working the short rows in the Heel and Toe, lift the wraps over before you lift the stitch over on the wrapped pegs to give the sock a cleaner look.

Heel Reinforcement

Once the Heel is complete, it is a good idea to add extra reinforcement to each side.

Work the stitch on the adjacent peg to the starting peg and last peg of the Heel. The adjacent pegs are not one of the heel pegs. Pick up the stitch on the row below, located at base of inside of the peg. Place the stitch on the adjacent peg or starting peg and last peg of the Heel, leaving 2 loops. Be sure to lift both loops as you work those stitches on the next row.

FOOT

Continue working around the loom in pattern for the length of the Foot. The Foot length is determined by measuring the length of the Foot in inches and then subtracting 2" for the Toe.

TOE

The Toe is worked in short rows, the same as the Heel *(see Heel, page 5)*.

BINDING OFF

① Knit the first two pegs.

② Lift the loop off the second peg and place it onto the first peg, leaving the second peg empty.

③ Lift the bottom loop over the top loop and off the peg, placing it on the adjacent empty peg.

④ Knit the next peg. Place this loop on the peg to the right. Lift the bottom loop over the top loop and off the peg, placing it on the empty peg to the left.

⑤ Continue around to last peg.

⑥ Slip last loop off peg and cut yarn leaving an 18" tail for sewing. Slip the tail through the loop.

SEWING THE TOE

Sew the Toe closed using a yarn needle using the Invisible Stitch or the Whip Stitch as shown on the DVD. Start by threading the yarn needle with the long end. With the right sides or the outsides of the sock facing, line up the stitches on the top and bottom of the Toe.

Invisible Stitch

Bring the needle from behind the work and through the center of the first stitch next to the yarn end. Bring the needle over the top of the edges and pick up both loops of the corresponding stitch on the second piece. Bring the needle back over the edges and pick up the inverted "V" of the next stitch. Repeat this process across being careful to maintain even tension.

Grafting

Another method is to sew the seam without binding off. Thread a yarn needle with a length of waste yarn and slip half of the stitches off the pegs and onto the waste yarn. With a second length of waste yarn, repeat for the remaining half of the stitches. Thread a yarn needle with the tail and pick up the stitches from the waste yarn alternating from one side to the other. This will gently pull the 2 sides together. Once you have closed the toe seam securely, gently remove the waste yarn.

sizing

How do I determine the number of pegs based on foot size and width?

Measure around the ball of your foot or widest part at base of toes, with foot resting on floor. Multiply that number of inches by 7. Multiply this number by .85, which accounts for the stretch of the yarn. The resulting number is the number of pegs that should be used for your sock. If you get an uneven number, add 1 to arrive at an even number of pegs to be able to work a rib pattern.

How many pegs do I cast on?

For Width: Measure around the ball of foot.

7" = approximately 42 pegs
8" = approximately 48 pegs
9" = approximately 54 pegs

For Length: The length of sock is based on number of rounds worked.

Just remember the toe adds approximately 2" to the length of the sock, so measure accordingly when determining the foot length.

Remember these numbers are approximates. Use larger amount of pegs for very wide feet or very large ankles. Use the ribbing stitch for very thin feet and legs. You will find your proper sizing very quickly, and can rely on instructions within specific patterns.

Resizing a Sock Pattern

Most sock patterns are written for a specific size, but you can adjust to the size desired and still use the pattern that you have chosen.

Remember, the size around the opening of the sock is determined by how many pegs you cast on. Be sure to increase or decrease the number of pegs used by a multiple of the pattern used. For example, If your pattern is using 2 knit and 2 purl stitches for a rib pattern, you will need to increase or decrease by a multiple of 4 stitches in order maintain the pattern.

Work as many rows or inches as desired for the length of the sock. For example, if the pattern says to work in knit stitch for 3 inches or 15 rounds and you want the sock longer to the knee, you can continue work as many rows until you've reached the desired length. Similarly, after working the heel, you can shorten or lengthen the foot of the sock by adjusting the number of rounds or inches you work before starting the toe.

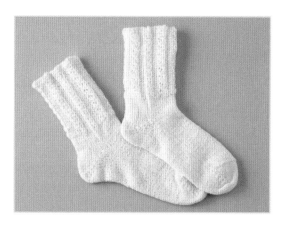

mock cable
socks

This cute cabled sock will please the little girl in your life. Don't be intimidated; the mock cable is easy to knit. And, while it is sized for children, it can easily be resized to fit any foot as long as the cast on is a multiple of 6 stitches.

materials

Knitting Loom: KB Sock Loom

Stitches: FS, PS and Cable

Yarn: 150 yards of fingering weight yarn. Red Heart® Heart & Sole™ (Ivory) was used in sample.

SUPER FINE 1

Notions: Knitting tool, Tapestry needle, Cable needle (optional), (2) pieces of contrasting color yarn, each 10" long (optional) for closing toe.

GAUGE: 7 stitches and 12 rounds = 1" in FS.

LEFT CROSS (abbreviated LC)

The Left Cross worked over two knit stitches in the K3, P3 rib. To knit the Left Cross, knit to the two pegs where the cross will take place. Take the yarn behind the first peg and knit the second stitch. Place this stitch on a cable needle and let it hang in the middle of the loom or hold it with your fingers. Move the skipped stitch over to the empty peg to the left. Place the held stitch on the first peg to the right. Knit the second stitch. Left Cross completed.

mock cable pattern
(Multiple of 6)

Round 1: P3, K3 around the loom.

Round 2: P3, LC (over first 2 knit stitches), K1. Repeat around the loom.

Round 3: P3, K3 around the loom.

Round 4: P3, K1, LC (over last 2 knit stitches); repeat around the loom.

Repeat these 4 rounds for pattern.

instructions

Size: 6½" foot circumference (child age 5 to 6) and a leg length of approx. 4" *(see Sizing, page 7)*.

1. CO 42 pegs, using the Cable Cast On *(see Casting On, page 3)*.

2. Work in Mock Cable Pattern for 36 rounds (9 repeats) or to desired length.

3. Knit in FS for 12 rounds.

4. Turn heel on 21 pegs, using short row shaping *(see Heel, page 5 or as shown in the DVD)*. There will be 7 unwrapped pegs when finished decreasing.

5. Knit in FS for a total of 45 rounds, or until knitting reaches the base of the big toe.

6. Repeat Heel instructions for toe. Sew or weave toe closed *(see Sewing the Toe, page 7)*.

diagonal rib dancing
socks

This is a fun sock that works well with both striped and solid-color yarns. It starts out using 55 pegs for the cuff and then you increase to 56 pegs for the rest of the sock. The one peg increase is explained at the beginning of the Leg instructions. Read the instructions carefully before beginning leg.

materials

Knitting Loom: KB Sock Loom

Stitches: KS and PS

Yarn: 203 yards of fingering weight yarn. Bernat® Sox (Crazy Hot) was used in sample.

SUPER FINE 1

Notions: Knitting tool, Tapestry needle, (2) pieces of contracting color yarn, each 10" long (optional) for closing toe.

GAUGE: 7 stitches and 12 rounds = 1" in KS.

instructions

Size: 9" foot circumference and a leg length of approx. 7¹/₂" *(see Sizing, page 7)*.

To Begin: Set your loom for 56 pegs. Cast On using the E-wrap Cast On *(see Casting On, page 2)*.

1. CO 55 pegs beginning with the **second** peg from the starting peg. **This will leave the first peg unwrapped while you work on the Cuff.** You will work across the corner, skipping this empty peg as you work the cuff. Work KS for 1 round.

2. **Cuff:** This is Rib stitch with 5 peg multiples on your 55 cast on pegs. K3, P2 around for 1¹/₂". Work KS for 1 more round.

3 Leg:
Before you begin the first Leg round, work 1 peg Increase so that you have a total of 56 pegs.

To Increase, reach in between the peg 1 and 55 with your hook, pick up the loop between the pegs and place it on the empty peg. Pick up a second loop and place it on the same peg, to close up any hole that may form. You now have 56 pegs to work for the Leg.

diagonal garter stitch pattern (Multiple of 8)

Round 1: KS around the loom.

Round 2: K4, P4 around the loom.

Round 3: KS around the loom.

Round 4: K4, P4 around the loom.

Round 5: KS around the loom.

Round 6: K2, P4, K4, P4 around the loom to last 2 stitches, K2.

Round 7: KS around the loom.

Round 8: K2, P4, K4, P4 around the loom to last 2 stitches, K2.

Round 9: KS around the loom.

Round 10: P4, K4 around the loom.

Round 11: KS around the loom.

Round 12: P4, K4 around the loom.

Round 13: KS around the loom.

Round 14: P2, K4, P4, K4 around the loom to last 2 stitches P2.

Round 15: KS around the loom.

Round 16: P2, K4, P4, K4 around the loom to last 2 stitches P2.

Repeat these 16 rounds, 5 times. *See detailed graph of pattern at bottom of page.*

The leg will be approximately 6" long, not counting the cuff.

Graph of Rounds 1 thru 16 of Diagonal Garter Stitch Pattern:

■ = knit   ✪ = purl

								Round #
✪	✪	■	■	■	■	✪	✪	16
■	■	■	■	■	■	■	■	15
✪	✪	■	■	■	■	✪	✪	14
■	■	■	■	■	■	■	■	13
■	■	■	■	✪	✪	✪	✪	12
■	■	■	■	■	■	■	■	11
■	■	■	■	✪	✪	✪	✪	10
■	■	■	■	■	■	■	■	9
■	■	✪	✪	✪	✪	■	■	8
■	■	■	■	■	■	■	■	7
■	■	✪	✪	✪	✪	■	■	6
■	■	■	■	■	■	■	■	5
✪	✪	✪	✪	■	■	■	■	4
■	■	■	■	■	■	■	■	3
✪	✪	✪	✪	■	■	■	■	2
■	■	■	■	■	■	■	■	1

4 **Heel:** Turn heel on 28 pegs, using short row shaping *(see Heel, page 5 or as shown in the DVD)*. You will have 8 unwrapped pegs when finished decreasing.

When the Heel is complete, it is time to work the foot. You can work the foot in knit stitches only or you can work the Diagonal Garter Stitch pattern again when knitting across the top of the foot.

If continuing with Diagonal Garter Stitch you will want to use the KS for the sole side of the foot. The sole uses pegs 1-28 and the top of the foot uses pegs 29-56. Follow the directions below for making the foot if continuing with the pattern used for the leg.

5 **Foot:** Always work in KS on pegs 1-28 for sole of sock. When you reach peg 29, and if you are using the pattern on the instep (pegs 29-56) of the sock, work 16 rounds in pattern.
Repeat Rounds 10-16 from page 12.
Repeat Rounds 1-9 from page 12.

If you are not working the instep in pattern, work in KS for all stitches until foot is desired length.

6 **Toe:** Repeat Heel. Sew or weave toe closed *(see Sewing the Toe, page 7)*.

beaded cuff
socks

Add a little bling to your sock knitting with beads. It's easy to do, yet the results look impressive! With so many wonderful beads and yarns out there, the sky really is the limit. Once you get started, you'll want to add beads to everything!

materials

Knitting Loom: KB Sock Loom

Stitches: FS with adding beads and PS

Yarn: 290 yards of fingering weight yarn. Lion Brand® Sock-Ease™ (Grape Soda) was used in sample.

Notions: Knitting tool, Tapestry needle, Big eye beading needle, or any straight needle that will fit through the bead, 200 size 6/0 glass seed beads, (2) pieces of contrasting color yarn, each 10" long (optional) for closing toe.

GAUGE: 7 stitches and 11 rounds = 1" in FS.

beading

First, string the number of beads needed onto the yarn. The easiest way to do this is to purchase a Big eye beading needle. It is a needle that is made of wire, and the eye runs the whole length of the needle. You will be able to thread your yarn directly into this needle. If you don't have a needle of this type, then use a straight needle whose eye is small enough to fit through the bead. Thread the needle with a strong thread and tie it into a small loop. Place the end of your yarn through this loop and let it hang over a few inches. Thread the beads by slipping them over the needle and thread and down onto the yarn.

1 To place the beads in the knitting, knit to the peg where the bead is to be added. Push the bead up to the knitting as close as you can.

2 Lift the stitch off the peg where the bead is to be placed.

3 Take the working yarn with the bead behind this peg.

4 Replace the stitch on the peg. Knit the next stitch as normal. You will not be knitting the actual stitch where the bead is placed. Continue adding beads in this manner as directed by the pattern.

Tip: It is a good idea to rewind your yarn before stringing the beads onto it. This will help you to avoid running into knots or other defects in the yarn that would cause problems with stringing the beads.

beaded rib (Multiple of 5)

Round 1: K3, P2 around the loom.

Round 2: K1, place bead, K1, P2. Repeat around the loom.

Round 3: K3, P2 around the loom.

Round 4: K3, P2 around the loom.

Repeat these 4 rounds for pattern.

instructions

Size: 8¹/₂" foot circumference (an average woman's size 8). These can be sized up or down as long as a multiple of 5 is used *(see Sizing, page 7)*.

1 String 100 beads onto your yarn.

2 CO 50 pegs, using the Cable Cast On *(see Casting On, page 3)*.

3 Knit in Beaded Rib for 40 rounds (10 repeats).

4 Knit 20 rounds in FS.

5 Turn Heel on 25 pegs, using short row *(see Heel, page 5 or as shown in the DVD)*. You will have 9 unwrapped pegs when finished decreasing.

6 Knit in FS for a total of 70 rounds, or until knitting reaches base of the big toe.

7 Repeat Heel instructions for Toe. Sew or weave Toe closed *(see Sewing the Toe, page 7)*.

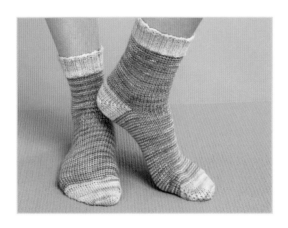

springtime stripes
socks

The colors in these socks remind me of the first spring crocuses. The green and purple swirl around each other in perfect one-row stripes. Change the colors to blue and yellow for summer, red and orange for fall, or blue and white for winter. You could even plan the color scheme around a favorite holiday. Whatever colors you choose, these socks are fun and easy to knit.

materials

Knitting Loom: KB Sock Loom

Stitches: KS, PS and FS

Yarn: 190 yards of Color A (green) and 145 yards of Color B (purple) of fingering weight yarn.
Knit Picks Stroll Tonal (Springtime and Blue Violet) was used in sample.

Notions: Knitting tool, Tapestry needle, (2) pieces of contrasting color yarn, each 10" long (optional) for sewing toe.

GAUGE: 7 stitches and 12 rounds = 1" in FS.

instructions

Size: 8½" foot circumference (an average woman's size 8) and a leg length of approx. 6" *(see Sizing, page 7)*.

1. With Color A (green), CO 52 pegs, using the Cable Cast On *(see Casting On, page 3)*.

2. K2, P2 for 16 rounds, or desired length.

3. Work in FS for 1 round.

4. Attach Color B (purple); Do not cut Color A. Work in FS for 1 round with CB.

5. Drop Color B and with Color A, work in FS for 1 round.

6. Repeat steps four and five 26 times more (total of 54 rounds), or until desired length, ending with Color A. Do not cut Color B.

7. With Color A, turn heel on 26 pegs, using short row shaping *(see Heel, page 5 or as shown in the DVD)*. You will have 8 unwrapped pegs when finished decreasing.

8. Knit in FS for 1 round with Color B. This will be the first full round after turning the heel.

9. Drop Color B and with Color A, work in FS for 1 round.

10. Repeat steps eight and nine 34 times more (total of 70 rounds), or until knitting reaches base of the big toe, ending with Color A. Cut Color B leaving a tail for weaving in.

11. With Color A, repeat Heel instructions for Toe. Sew or weave toe closed *(see Sewing the Toe, page 7)*.

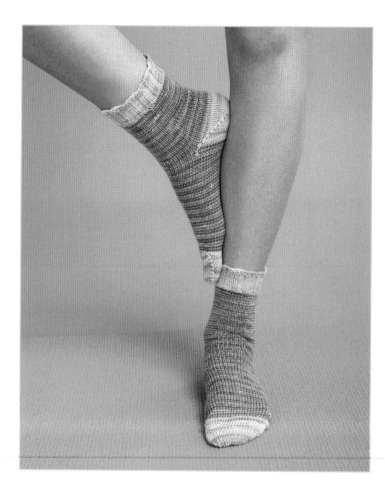

Tips:

To help keep the yarns from getting tangled, place one ball of yarn on your right side and other ball on your left side.

When starting a round with a new color do NOT twist the yarns around each other.

When you reach the last 3 stitches of the round, hold on to the yarn of the previous color so that the stitches will not be too loose when knitted over. Do not pull the last stitch too tight; keep it the same tension as the other stitches.

Because of the changing of colors, when knitting the first full round after the heel, the last peg of the round will have a stitch and a wrap on it. On this first round, just knit the stitch and leave the wrap. On the next round, knit the stitch and the wrap together. This only applies to the heel. When knitting the toe, knit the wrap and stitch together as you normally would.

pedicure
socks

These pedicure socks are easy to knit and can liven up even the gloomiest day. Make them long or short, loud or quiet; it's up to you. Using only Stockinette Stitch, Flat Stitch and Knit Stitch, these are great for any skill level. Get ready to show off those toes!

materials

Knitting Loom: KB Sock Loom

Stitches: FS and KS

Yarn: 220 yards of fingering weight yarn. Knit Picks Stroll Hand Painted (Juice Box) was used in sample.

SUPER FINE 1

Notions: Knitting tool, Tapestry needle, (2) pieces of contrasting color yarn, each 10" long (optional) for closing toe.

GAUGE: 7 stitches and 12 rows = 1" in FS.

instructions

Size: 8½" foot circumference (an average woman's size 8) *(see Sizing, page 7)*.

1 CO 50 pegs, using the E-wrap Cast On *(see Casting On, page 2)*.

2 Knit 15 rounds in FS.

3 Knit 1 round using KS.

4 Eyelet Round: Lift the loops from all odd numbered pegs and place them on the even numbered pegs. All the odd numbered pegs will be empty and the even number pegs will have 2 loops. Wrap the round using the KS. The odd pegs will have 1 wrap, the even pegs will have 3 wraps. Lift over, only lifting over the pegs that have 3 wraps, and lifting the bottom 2 over the top 1. All pegs should now have 1 wrap.

5 Knit 1 round in KS.

6 Knit 15 round in FS.

7 Reach inside the loom and find the CO edge. The stitches will be loopy. Find the loop that is attached to the yarn tail and place the loop over the first peg. Continue around the loom until all the pegs have 2 loops on them. Lift the bottom loop over the top. Hemmed Cuff is completed.

8 Knit 30 rounds in FS, or desired length.

9 Turn Heel using short row shaping *(see Heel, page 5 or as shown in the DVD)*. There will be 9 unwrapped pegs when finished decreasing.

10 Knit 60 rounds in FS.

11 Knit 10 rounds in K3, P2 rib.

12 BO all pegs *(see Binding Off, page 6)*.

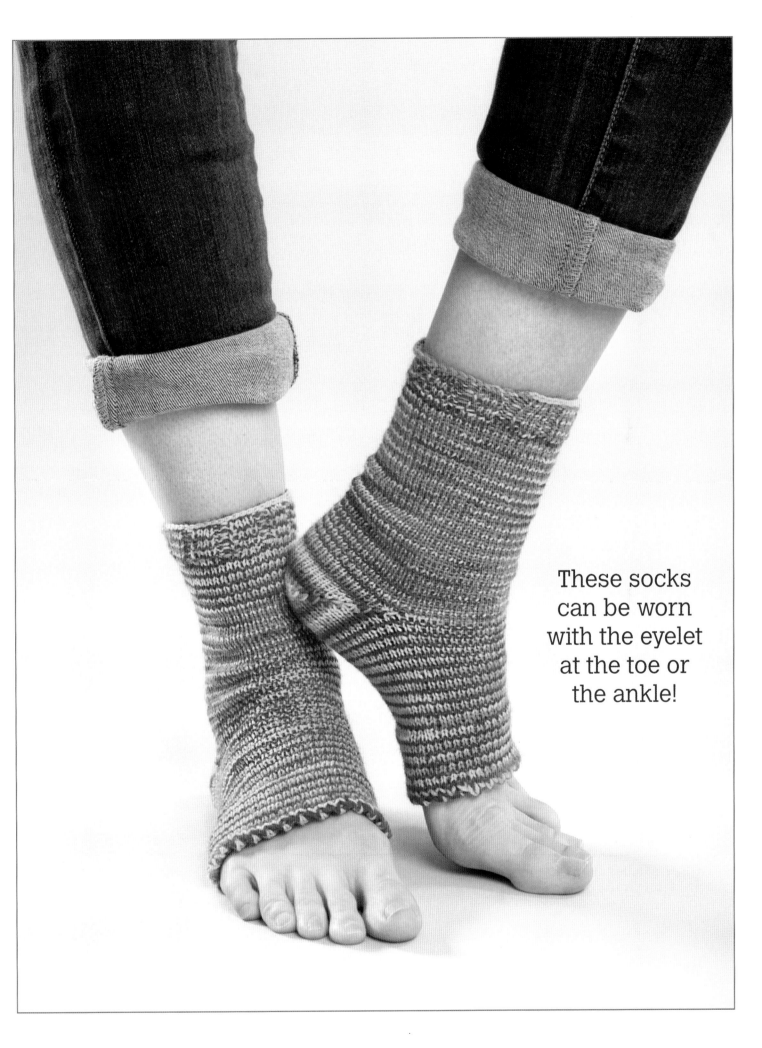

These socks can be worn with the eyelet at the toe or the ankle!

garter blocks
socks

Variegated yarn, an easy stitch pattern, and a rolled cuff make these socks fun to knit. Designed to fit your favorite tween to teen, they can easily be sized up or down to fit a variety of feet.

materials

Knitting Loom: KB Sock Loom

Stitches: FS, KS and PS

Yarn: 220 yards of fingering weight yarn. Knit Picks Stroll Multi (Cupcake Multi) was used in sample.

Notions: Knitting tool, Tapestry needle, (2) pieces of contrasting color yarn, each 10" long (optional) for sewing toe.

GAUGE: 7 stitches and 12 rounds = 1" in FS.

garter blocks pattern
(Multiple of 8)

Round 1: P4, K4 around the loom.

Round 2: Knit around the loom.

Rounds 3 and 4: Repeat Rounds 1 and 2.

Round 5: K4, P4 around the loom.

Round 6: Knit around the loom.

Round 7 and 8: Repeat Rounds 5 and 6.

Repeat these 8 rounds for pattern.

instructions

Size: Fits 8" foot circumference (approx. 12 to 14 year old) and a leg length of approx. 5" *(see Sizing, page 7)*.

1 CO 48 pegs, using the Cable Cast On *(see Casting On, page 3)*.

2 **Cuff:** Knit in FS for 10 rounds, or desired length. This will give you a rolled cuff.

3 **Leg:** Work in Garter Block Pattern for 56 rounds, or desired length. Work in FS for 10 rounds.

4 **Heel:** Turn Heel on 24 pegs, using short row shaping *(see Heel, page 5 or as shown in the DVD)*. You will have 8 unwrapped pegs when finished decreasing.

5 **Foot:** Knit in FS for 60 rounds, or until knitting reaches base of the big toe.

6 **Toe:** Repeat heel instructions. Sew or weave toe closed *(see Sewing the Toe, page 7)*.

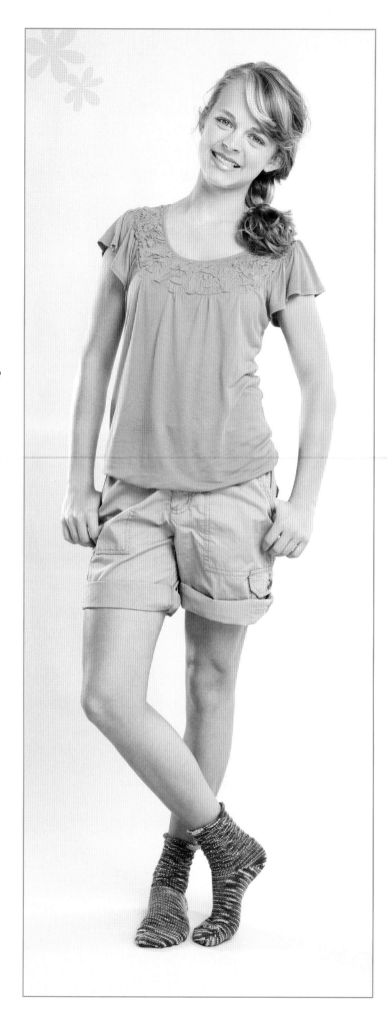

spiral tube
socks for preemies

These are great little socks for your tiniest one's feet. Made without heels, they are easy and quick to knit and can be sized up to fit any member of the family.

materials

Knitting Loom: KB Sock Loom

Stitches: FS and KS

Yarn: 45 yards of light weight yarn. Bernat® Baby Jacquards (Cherry Berry) was used in sample. Make sure to use a soft yarn, as preemie skin is very delicate.

Notions: Knitting tool, Tapestry needle, (2) pieces of contrasting color yarn, each 8" long (optional) for closing toe.

GAUGE: 7 stitches and 10 rounds = 1" in K2, P2 rib.

Note: Spiral tube socks have comfort-fit ribbing that give the socks enough stretch yet still fit comfortably even without a heel. These characteristics make the socks ideal for preemies, and newborns. Because there is no heel, they will fit a variety of foot lengths, and the ribbing helps it stay on those squirming baby feet.

knit spiral rib pattern

Rounds 1 to 6: K3, P3 around the loom.

Rounds 7 to 12: K2, then P3, K3 around the loom until last 4 stitches, end P3, K1.

Rounds 13 to 18: K1, then P3, K3 around the loom until last 5 stitches, end P3, K2.

Rounds 19 to 24: P3, K3 around the loom.

Rounds 25 to 30: P2, then K3, P3 around the loom until last 4 stitches, end K3, P1.

Rounds 31 to 36: P1, then K3, P3 around the loom until last 5 stitches, end K3, P2.

Resizing Socks

The length can be adjusted to your personal preference. To make the socks longer, after knitting Round 36, go back to Round 1 and start again. Keep repeating these 36 rounds until desired length. You may also stop before you have completed a 36 round repeat as long as you stop at the end of one of the 6 round sections. The cuff section may also be lengthened for adult socks (30 rounds would be a good amount) *(see Sizing, page 7)*.

instructions

Sizes: To fit a 2-4 pound preemie (6-12 mos).

1 CO 24 (30) pegs, using the Cable Cast On *(see Casting On, page 3)*.

2 Preemie Cuff: K2, P2 for 8 rounds.
Baby Cuff: K3, P3 for 2 rounds.

3 Preemie Socks: Knit Spiral Rib pattern 1 time (36 rounds).
Baby Socks: Knit Spiral Rib pattern 1 time (36 rounds) then repeat Rounds 1-24 one time, or desired length.

4 Both Sizes: Knit 1 round in Knit stitch.

5 Toe: Turn Toe on 12(15) pegs, using short row shaping *(see Toe, page 6 or as shown in the DVD)*. You will have 4(5) unwrapped pegs when finished decreasing.

6 Sew or weave toe closed *(see Sewing the Toe, page 7)*.

little preemie
hat

The KB Sock Loom isn't just for socks! This little preemie hat was knit using the sock loom adjusted to its largest setting. It is a quick project, uses little yarn, and would make a great gift or item for charity. Self-patterning yarn makes it extra special, though a solid color could be used as well.

materials

Knitting Loom: KB Sock Loom

Stitches: FS and KS

Yarn: 85 yards of light weight yarn. Bernat® Baby Jacquards (Cherry Berry) was used in the sample.

Notions: Knitting tool, Tapestry needle, Crochet hook (size E).

GAUGE: 6 stitches and 13 rounds = 1" in FS.

Tip: We suggest knitting a few rows with the chosen yarn, if different from the yarn used in the sample, to see how it knits up. You want the yarn to lift *very easily* over the pegs to make a soft hat. Also, test to see if a loop will stretch to an adjacent peg for the yarn overs. We've had very good results with Bernat Baby Jacquards.

instructions

Finished Size: Measures 10" in circumference and approx. 4¼" deep. This would fit a 2-4 pound preemie.

1. CO the entire loom (60 pegs) using the Cable Cast On *(see Casting On, page 3)*.

2. Work in the FS, until the hat measures 6" from the cast on edge, making sure that the last round is wrapped loosely.

3. **Eyelet round:** Lift the loop from one peg to a peg adjacent to it. Lift the loop from peg 1 onto peg 2. Peg 1 will be empty and peg 2 will have 2 loops on it. Starting with the peg that has 2 loops, count over 3 pegs. This will be peg 4. Lift the loop from peg 4 onto peg 5. Peg 4 will be empty and peg 5 will have 2 loops on it. Continue around the loom. You will have 2 pegs with loops between each empty peg.

4. After moving the loops, work this row with the FS, creating a new loop on each peg. Lift 2 loops over 1 on the pegs that have 3 loops, and 1 over 1 on those that have 2 loops. The pegs with just 1 loop (the previously empty pegs) will not be lifted over. When you are done, each peg should have 1 loop on it.

5. Knit 8 more rounds using the FS.

6. BO all pegs *(see Binding Off, page 6)*.

7. Crochet a chain approximately 14" long. Weave through eyelets, pull tight and tie into a bow. You could also make a braid, or use purchased ribbon in place of the chain.

8. Roll brim up so that it is even and hat length measures approx. 4¼", including the brim and excluding the knitting above the crocheted chain, and tack into place at each side edge.

horizontal rib
tippy toe socks

These are truly easy socks to make—they only look complex! You will get many compliments when you wear them. This pattern works well with solid or striped yarns.

materials

Knitting Loom: KB Sock Loom

Stitches: KS and PS

Yarn: 332 yards of fingering weight yarn. Paton's® Kroy Socks (Aqua Jacquard) was used in sample.

Notions: Knitting tool, Tapestry needle, (2) pieces of contrasting color yarn, each 10" long (optional) for closing toe.

GAUGE: 7 stitches and 12 rounds = 1" in KS.

horizontal rib pattern
(Multiple of 3+1)

Rounds 1-3: P1, K2 around the loom ending each round with a Purl.

Rounds 4 and 5: Purl around the loom.

Rounds 6-8: P1, K2 around the loom ending each round with a purl.

Round 9: Purl around the loom.

Rounds 10-12: P1, K2 around the loom ending each round with a purl.

Round 13: Purl around the loom.

Repeat these 13 rounds for pattern.

instructions

Size: Fits 8½" foot circumference *(see Sizing, page 7)*.

1. CO 52 pegs, using the Cable Cast On *(see Casting On, page 3).* Work one row in KS.

2. **Cuff:** Work in a K2, P2 pattern until the cuff is 1" long.

3. **Leg:** Repeat Rounds 1-13 of Horizontal Rib Pattern, 4 times; then repeat Rounds 1-4 once more (a total of 56 rounds).

4. **Heel:** Turn Heel on 26 pegs, using short row shaping *(see Heel, page 5 or as shown in the DVD).* The Heel is knit in KS or FS. You will have 8 unwrapped pegs when finished decreasing.

5. **Foot:** The Foot will be formed by knitting across the sole of the sock (pegs 1-25) in KS and continuing the Horizontal Rib Pattern across the instep of the sock (pegs 26-52). Repeat Horizontal Rib Pattern starting with Rounds 5-13. Repeat Round 1-13, 2 times more, working only on the top of foot (pegs 26-52). Pegs 1-25 should be continued in KS. Work Rounds 1-5 once more on entire sock.

6. **Toe:** Repeat Heel instructions. Sew or weave toe closed *(see Sewing the Toe, page 7).*

interrupted
rib socks

This easy sock consists of a four-row repeat, two of which are simply Knit Stitch. This is a variation of the K2, P2 rib and would work great with solid or variegated yarn. It is easy to size up or down for any foot.

materials

Knitting Loom: KB Sock Loom

Stitches: KS, FS and PS

Yarn: 285 yards of fingering weight yarn. Knit Picks Essential Kettle Hand-Dyed (Spruce) was used in sample.

Notions: Knitting tool, Tapestry needle, (2) pieces of contrasting color yarn, each 10" long (optional) for closing toe.

GAUGE: 7 stitches and 12 rounds = 1" in FS.

interrupted rib pattern
(Multiple of 4)

Rounds 1 and 2: K2, P2 around the loom.

Round 3 and 4: Knit around the loom.

Repeat these 4 rounds for pattern.

instructions

Size: 8½" foot circumference (an average woman's size 8) and a leg length of approx. 6" *(see Sizing, page 7)*.

1 CO 52 pegs, using the Cable Cast On *(see Casting On, page 3)*.

2 **Cuff:** K2, P2 for 13 rounds, or desired length.

3 **Leg:** Work in Interrupted Rib Pattern for 60 rounds, or desired length. Knit in FS for 10 rounds.

4 **Heel:** Turn Heel on 26 pegs, using short row shaping *(see Heel, page 5 or as shown in the DVD)*. There will be 8 unwrapped pegs when finished decreasing.

5 **Foot:** Knit in FS for a total of 70 rounds, or until knitting reaches base of the big toe.

6 **Toe:** Repeat Heel instructions. Sew or weave toe closed *(see Sewing the Toe, page 7)*.

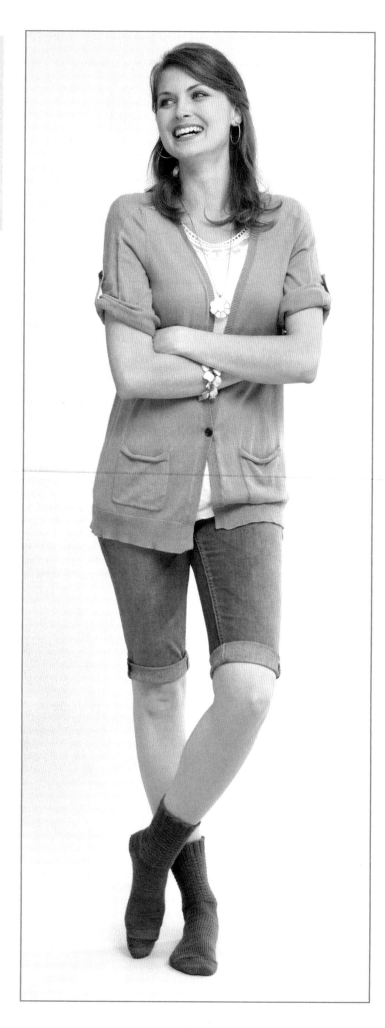

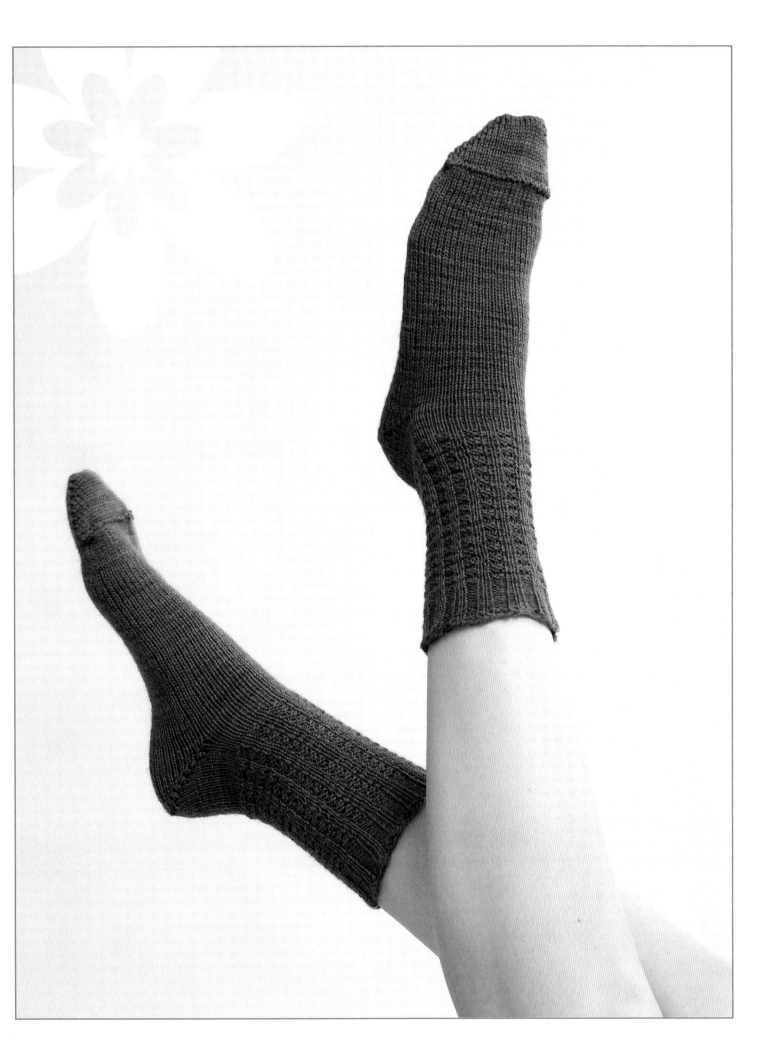

men's ribbed
socks

These classic ribbed socks are perfect for the men in your life.

Simple and unfussy, they are easy to knit and sure to please.

materials

Knitting Loom: KB Sock Loom

Stitches: FS, KS and PS

Yarn: 325 yards of fingering weight yarn. Knit Picks Stroll Tonal (Kindling) was used in sample.

Notions: Knitting tool, Tapestry needle, (2) pieces of contrasting color yarn, each 10" long (optional) for closing toe.

GAUGE: 7 stitches and 12 rounds = 1" in FS.

rib pattern

(Multiple of 4)

Round 1: K2, P2 around the loom.

Repeat this round for pattern.

instructions

Size: 9" foot circumference (an average man's size 8½ to 9) and a leg length of approx. 7" *(see Sizing, page 5)*.

1 CO 56 pegs, using the Cable Cast On *(see Casting On, page 3)*.

2 Leg: K2, P2 for 80 rounds, or desired length.

3 Heel: Turn Heel on 28 pegs, using short row shaping *(see Heel, page 5 or as shown in the DVD)*. The heel is knit in FS. You will have 8 unwrapped pegs when finished decreasing.

4 Foot: Knit for a total of 75 rounds, or until knitting reaches the base of the big toe. To create the ribbing just on the top of the sock and the FS on the sides and sole of the sock, you will use both K2, P2 and the FS in each of the 75 rounds. This means the first half of the stitches or the heel stitches will continue in FS. The second half of the stitches will stay with the ribbing K2, P2 as established to maintain a continued flow of the ribbing.

5 Knit all stitches, top and sole, in FS for 2 rounds.

6 Toe: Repeat Heel instructions. The toe is knit in FS. Sew or weave toe closed *(see Sewing the Toe, page 7)*.

We have made every effort to ensure that these instructions are accurate and complete. We cannot, however, be responsible for human error, typographical mistakes, or variations in individual work.

production team

Instructional Editor: Linda A. Daley
Contributors: Faith Schmidt, Cindy Mott, Pat Novak, and Kim Novak
Editorial Writer: Susan McManus Johnson
Senior Graphic Artist: Lora Puls
Graphic Artists: Katherine Laughlin and Becca Snider
Photo Stylist: Angela Alexander
Photographer: Jason Masters

Copyright © 2011 by Leisure Arts, Inc., 104 Champs Blvd., STE 100, Maumelle, Arkansas 72113 www.leisurearts.com. All rights reserved. This publication is protected under federal copyright laws. Reproduction or distribution of this publication or any other Leisure Arts publication, including publications which are out of print, is prohibited unless specifi cally authorized. This includes, but is not limited to, any form of reproduction or distribution on or through the Internet, including posting, scanning, or e-mail transmission.